WITH

URBAN ENTREPRENEUR

FOOD

Urban Entrepreneur: Food

Scobre Educational
2255 Calle Clara
La Jolla, CA 92037

Scobre Operations & Administration
42982 Osgood Road
Fremont, CA 94539

www.scobre.com
info@scobre.com

Scobre Educational publications may be purchased for
educational, business, or sales promotional use.

Cover and layout design by Jana Ramsay
Copyedited by Susan Sylvia
Some photos by Getty Images

ISBN: 978-1-61570-517-7

TABLE OF CONTENTS

Chapter 1	Pat's or Geno's?	4
Chapter 2	Twitter, Tacos, and Korean BBQ	12
Chapter 3	Tonnie's Minis	20
Chapter 4	Summer in the City	29
Chapter 5	The Entrepreneur of Tomorrow	36

Chapter 1
Pat's or Geno's?

It's a Saturday night in Philadelphia. The weather is cool and crisp; a perfect October evening. The entire city is buzzing with activity. Everybody is out because there's just so much to do.

Some friends are hanging out, having a good time. They've been chillin', listening to music, and shooting hoops over at the YMCA. Somebody says he's hungry.

There is a *market* for late-night restaurants and food joints. In this case, the word market means a *need*, or an *opportunity*. That's where the entrepreneur comes in. Smart entrepreneurs observe what's going on around them. Then, they fill a need, and create the opportunity to make money for themselves.

Everybody agrees. It doesn't matter that it's close to midnight. The city lifestyle is all about working late, playing late, and even eating late. Time for a Philly-style cheesesteak.

They all know where they're headed. To south Philly, the corner of 9th Street and Passyunk Avenue. But the really important question hasn't been answered yet: Pat's or Geno's?

These sandwich shops are located right

Geno's restaurant lights up at night. This place was made for late-night eating!

Pat's and Geno's cheesesteaks are slightly different. At Pat's, chopped steak is served topped with Cheez Whiz. Geno's steaks are served thinly sliced, and they recommend provolone cheese.

across the street from each other. They are two of the most famous late-night restaurants in the city. Each one claims that it has the most delicious cheesesteak. Of course, this means they are natural rivals.

Pat's King of Steaks has been around for more than 80 years. It was started way back in the early 1930s. The owners were Pat Olivieri and his brother Harry. They were born in Philly, and they became entrepreneurs at a young age.

The brothers started out by opening a hot dog stand. So why isn't the restaurant called *Pat's King of Hot Dogs*? It was lunchtime, one day in 1933. Pat and his brother Harry were getting hungry. They were probably getting tired of eating their own hot dogs

The lunchtime rush at Pat's looks intense, but don't let that scare you away. Service is *quick*, and they keep the line moving.

every day. On that particular day, they felt like having a sandwich. So Harry ran out to the market and bought some steak and some rolls. The brothers chopped up the steak and some onions, and threw them on the grill.

Pat and Harry finished preparing their sandwiches and were ready to eat lunch. At that exact moment, a cab driver happened to pull up. He had planned to get a hot dog. But when he smelled the delicious aroma of steak, he asked if he could buy the steak sandwich instead. Thus, the famous Philly cheesesteak was born. (Well, almost – the cheese wasn't added until later). Pat and Harry were entrepreneurs who jumped on a great business idea, and it has been paying off ever since.

Geno's, Pat's competition, has also been around for a long time. It was started by a young entrepreneur named Joey Vento in the 1960s. Like Pat and Harry, he was born in the big city of Philadelphia. Joey always knew that he wanted to be in the food business. So, at a young age, he went to work for his father's restaurant. Later on, he opened up his own restaurant and named it Geno's.

A Geno's cheesesteak is slightly different than Pat's. Still, they are both delicious. You can't go wrong with delicious fresh bread filled with tender grilled steak, onions, and melting cheese.

Anyone who loves food would be lucky to live in a big city like Philadelphia. Whether you eat at Pat's or walk across the street to Geno's, you're in for a major treat, brought to you by some very successful entrepreneurs.

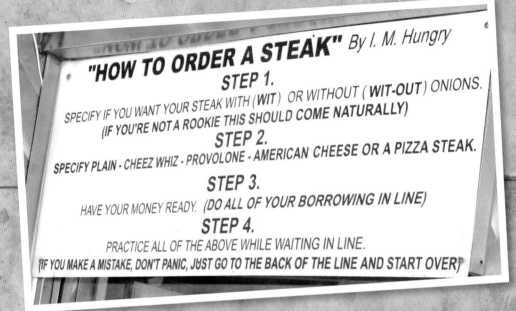

"HOW TO ORDER A STEAK" By I. M. Hungry

STEP 1.
SPECIFY IF YOU WANT YOUR STEAK WITH (WIT) OR WITHOUT (WIT-OUT) ONIONS. (IF YOU'RE NOT A ROOKIE THIS SHOULD COME NATURALLY)

STEP 2.
SPECIFY PLAIN - CHEEZ WHIZ - PROVOLONE - AMERICAN CHEESE OR A PIZZA STEAK.

STEP 3.
HAVE YOUR MONEY READY. (DO ALL OF YOUR BORROWING IN LINE)

STEP 4.
PRACTICE ALL OF THE ABOVE WHILE WAITING IN LINE.
(IF YOU MAKE A MISTAKE, DON'T PANIC, JUST GO TO THE BACK OF THE LINE AND START OVER)

The sandwiches may be different, but one thing is the same whether you end up at Pat's or at Geno's: you better know how to order. The lines are always long, and people will hassle you if you take too much time. There are very specific ways to order.

Chapter 2
Twitter, Tacos, and Korean BBQ

Los Angeles is a huge city, one of the biggest in the world. People of all ethnic backgrounds live there. Take Mark Manguera, for instance. Mark is Filipino, and he is married to a Korean woman. As a diversely populated city, Los Angeles has a market for many different foods. Just a few years ago, Mark was enjoying a carne asada taco. It would become the most important meal of his entire life. Suddenly, while eating, a thought entered his mind. *Somebody should*

put Korean Barbeque on a taco. Being married to a Korean woman, Mark had eaten Korean barbeque many times. He knew how delicious it was. He wasn't sure if anybody would want to eat a Korean Barbeque taco. But it seemed like an interesting idea that somebody should try.

So Mark sprang into action. He learned about the restaurant business. He found a business partner. Then he put together a menu. Mark understood an important fact: Entrepreneurs never wait for someone else to do something. What makes you an entrepreneur is when *you* are that someone else. For Mark, the result was the Kogi Korean BBQ taco truck.

Food trucks are common in big cities like LA, and you will find them in many other parts of the country, too. Sometimes they go to construction sites during workers'

The Kogi Korean BBQ truck is a favorite with the lunch crowd everywhere it goes!

lunch breaks, or park right outside big office buildings.

At first, food trucks sold basic things. You could find foods like sandwiches, soup, eggs, and coffee. Today, in cities like Los Angeles, food trucks sell many different types of food. You might find Indian food on one truck, and healthy organic food on another.

As an entrepreneur, Mark realized that there was a lot of competition. Sure, his Korean BBQ tacos were delicious. But this was a brand new idea. How would people find out about it?

The answer was social media. Mark and his employees started using Twitter. They spread the word about a delicious new food truck called the Kogi Korean BBQ taco truck. Their tweets would tell where the truck was going every day. They also offered discounts and lunch specials. This was a brilliant business idea, and it worked better than Mark could have dreamed. The BBQ truck has nearly 100,000 followers on Twitter. Every day, the truck shows up at the tweeted location. It's not uncommon for hundreds of people to be waiting for it!

The Kogi Korean BBQ truck offers food and a venue that is hip and new – different than a normal, everyday restaurant. It's exciting to track the truck on Twitter. And then, when you get there, you're hanging out with people who had the same idea as you.

The classic Kogi Short Rib taco.

Mark Manguera became a successful entrepreneur. He came up with a winning concept, and turned it into something exciting. Kogi Korean BBQ is a successful venture that came out of nowhere while Mark was eating a taco. When you're an entrepreneur, you never know when inspiration will strike.

America was built on a type of system, *capitalism*, which lets people work for the purpose of making money. This is key. Without capitalism, there would be no entrepreneurs. People would have no motivation to invent a product, or start a business. After all, if you knew you couldn't make money, you wouldn't even bother trying! There would be no Pat's or Geno's cheesesteaks, and no Kogi Korean BBQ taco truck.

Unfortunately, that's actually how it is in some countries. Governments have

When people think about capitalism, New York is often the first thing that comes to mind. It's the home of Wall Street, which is the financial center of the world. Many rich and powerful people, such as Donald Trump, live in New York City.

the power to control the way people do business. Instead of allowing entrepreneurs to try new things, the government tells people what kind of business they can run. It controls what prices can be charged. It also decides how much money is paid to employees.

Isn't it better to let people decide how they want to run a business? Fortunately for Tonnie Rozier, that is the American way. A true American entrepreneur, Tonnie started his very own business in New York City.

Tonnie was born and raised in an area of New York called Harlem. You might have heard of it – Harlem is known for its rich African-American culture and historic buildings. Many famous people were born there, like Sean "P. Diddy" Combs, basketball legend Kareem Abdul-Jabbar, and Roc-A-Fella co-founder Damon Dash.

P. Diddy

Kareem Abdul-Jabbar

Damon Dash

Harlem is also an area that suffers from poverty and crime. Tonnie could never have predicted that he would become so successful in his hometown one day.

When Tonnie was very young, he enjoyed spending time with his grandmother. She taught him all the secrets of baking mouth-watering cookies and cupcakes.

Tonnie learned so much from her that, by the time he was an adult, people were always asking him for his cookies. So he started charging two dollars and fifty cents for each bag. The response was huge. Before he knew it, he was selling fifty bags of cookies a day.

Tonnie decided to take advantage of his talent for baking. He figured that he could turn this skill into an actual career. He quit his job with the New York City Housing Authority and opened a tiny cupcake shop in

Greenwich Village. He named the shop Tonnie's Minis.

Tonnie Rozier was now the owner of a small business. He had become an entrepreneur. Thanks to America's capitalist system, Tonnie was free to set up a business exactly the way he wanted to. And other people were free to choose whether or not they wanted to spend their money on cupcakes. If they did, Tonnie would succeed. If not, his business would fail.

After opening his shop, Tonnie joined the ranks of thousands of other American entrepreneurs. They have opened drugstores, gas stations, hardware stores, 7-11s, and restaurants all over the country.

Luckily for Tonnie, his cupcakes were delicious, and also fairly priced. The treats sold very well, and became very popular. The only problem was that his shop was tiny. Tonnie knew he needed to expand. A large space was available in Harlem. The rent wasn't too expensive. There would be plenty of room to open up a new cupcake shop. Harlem, however, wasn't a rich area. There was no guarantee that people would continue

In a capitalist system, nothing is guaranteed. Just because one store or restaurant—or cupcake shop—succeeds, that doesn't mean that another one will.

to spend their money on cupcakes.

Tonnie had a big decision to make. Finally, he decided to take the risk. Having grown up in Harlem, he knew the area well. He had friends and relatives there. He knew that people enjoyed sweet treats like cupcakes. There were other bakeries and places that sold cupcakes, but he had confidence in himself and in his shop.

In business, sometimes a gamble pays off. And in Tonnie's case, it did. Tonnie's Minis in Harlem has been a major success. His cupcakes are so popular that sometimes there are even lines out the door. Tonnie Rozier's business was a huge success, all thanks to America's capitalist system and Tonnie's bold entrepreneurship.

Tonnie's cupcake shop in Harlem.

Chapter 4
Summer in the City

It's summertime in the city. Another fun, lazy day – but outside, it's crazy hot. The sun is beating down on the concrete. It makes you feel like you're walking on burning coals.

All of a sudden you hear a familiar sound coming from around the corner. It's the neighborhood ice cream truck.

After a game outside on a hot summer day, who doesn't want something refreshing?

On a blazing summer afternoon, an icy-cold, lemon Popsicle sounds very tempting. Or maybe you decide to ditch the ice cream truck and simply grab an ice cream sandwich from the freezer. Ice cream trucks, Popsicles, freezers – who came up with these things? How did they become useful and mainstream? These products exist because of smart and creative entrepreneurs. They notice how people live and what they want, and then they come up with ways to fulfill those needs.

Entrepreneurs come in all shapes, sizes, ages, and nationalities. As a matter of fact, the

Entrepreneurs understand capitalism and how to make money. In Tonnie Rozier's case, it was cupcakes. In a big city like Philadelphia, it was late-night places to eat. The entrepreneur is always looking around. If there is a need for something, the entrepreneur will fill that need.

entrepreneur who invented the Popsicle was only 11 years old. Way back in 1905, a San Francisco kid named Frank Epperson was hanging out on his back porch before bed. It was a cool evening, and he was drinking a glass of fruit-flavored soda, stirring the drink with a stick. Frank accidentally left the glass outside, and it stayed there overnight, with the stick still inside.

Frank was in for a major surprise the next morning. It can get very cold in San Francisco, especially during the winter. His sweet drink had frozen to the stick and turned into a delicious treat. At only 11 years old, he had invented the world's first Popsicle.

Years down the road, after Frank realized the value of this idea, he sold his invention to a big company. They started creating Popsicles for the entire world.

1905 was a long time ago, but Frank's invention is just as important today.

Actually, you can go back even further in time, and you'll find entrepreneurs who brought us products we still use today.

In 1897, there was an entrepreneur named Jerome Monroe Smucker. Does that name sound familiar? Mr. Smucker began selling a product called apple butter. There weren't even cars yet, so he would go door to door.

Smucker's first product: apple butter.

Smucker's has been turning fresh fruit into delicious jams and jellies since 1897.

Mr. Smucker would sell his apple butter straight from a wagon, which was pulled by a horse.

That was the beginning of a famous company that is still around today. The J.M. Smucker Company has always been a leader in jam and jelly – who hasn't eaten Smucker's jam at some point? But they also make many other food products. In 2002, Smucker's acquired Jif. This is one of America's favorite peanut butter brands. You've probably enjoyed a lot of PB&J sandwiches in your life. Chances are good that both the peanut butter and the jelly were Smucker's brands.

Nearly one billion dollars of peanut butter is sold every year, and that's just in the United States. People all over the world enjoy peanut butter. Seems like Jerome Monroe Smucker knew exactly what he was doing.

Chapter 5
The Entrepreneur of Tomorrow

Have you ever eaten at the Olive Garden or Red Lobster? Those restaurants are owned by a company named Darden Restaurants, which owns over a thousand restaurants. They rake in more than six billion dollars every year. Clarence Otis, Jr., is the CEO (chief executive officer) of Darden, and he is one of the most important people in the company. But success didn't come easily to Clarence.

He had to beat the odds to make it to such an important position. In the process, he blazed a trail that should inspire any entrepreneur.

Clarence grew up in Watts, an urban area in Los Angeles. Some people thought he was just a poor kid from the inner city. When Clarence was young, he used to get stopped and questioned by police, just because of the color of his skin. It was probably hard to imagine that one day he would become one of the most powerful African-American executives in the food business. Many entrepreneurs are people like Clarence—they have overcome challenges and stayed focused on their goals and dreams. Even from a young age, Clarence was determined to make something of his life. Ironically, Clarence didn't start out working in the food industry. Instead, he went to college and earned a law degree. Eventually Clarence ended up working for

Clarence Otis, Jr. won a scholarship to Williams College, in Massachusetts.

Darden Restaurants. Because of his outstanding performance, he was promoted to the position of CEO less than 10 years later, in 2004. He is now a respected executive and economic leader.

The future of the food business holds great promise, because food is one of the few things that no one

Being the CEO of a major corporation is a very well-paying job. According to Forbes magazine, in 2011 Clarence earned over $4 million.

can live without. There will be chances for a lot of people to become successful entrepreneurs in this industry: from the farmer who grows the food, to the restaurant or supermarket that sells it, and for everyone in between. And that includes you—the entrepreneur of tomorrow.

Are you ready?